CRYPTIDS AND MYSTERIOUS CREATURES:

FAKES OR MYSTERIES OF NATURE TO BE SOLVED?

Magnus Olivier

CONTENTS

CRYPTIDS AND MYSTERIOUS CREATURES: FAKES OR MYSTERIES OF NATURE TO BE SOLVED?

Magnus Olivier

INTRODUCTION

In the shadows of reality, in the darkest corners of the human imagination, mysterious creatures lurk that defy understanding and spark the curiosity of those willing to venture beyond the known. This book, "Cryptids and Mysterious Creatures: Fakes or Unsolved Mysteries of Nature?", invites readers to immerse themselves in a fascinating journey through legends and close encounters with beings that defy the laws of nature.

On each page, we will explore the narratives that have endured through the centuries, from ancient legends of sea monsters to modern reports of encounters with humanoid creatures in the most remote forests. Are these creatures real, manifestations of human creativity, or simply carefully crafted hoaxes?

As we enter the dark realm of cryptids, we will face the eternal question: Fakes or mysteries of nature to be solved? Through intriguing stories, detailed descriptions, and critical analysis, we will strive to shed light on these enigmatic presences that have left their mark on folklore, popular culture, and personal experiences.

Prepare for a journey that will challenge your perceptions

and take you to the limits of the unknown. Let us enter together into the darkness, where mysterious creatures wait, ready to reveal their secrets or to wrap us in the veil of mystery that surrounds them. Are we dealing with myths and legends, or are there unusual creatures still waiting to be discovered? The answer, dear readers, may lie in the pages you are about to explore. Welcome to a world where reality and fantasy intertwine in an intriguing and enigmatic embrace!

After a short review of what is and is not a cryptid and the competing theories that we find today, here you will find these mysteries:

Bigfoot (Sasquatch): An ape-like creature said to live in forested areas of North America.

Chupacabra: A being that feeds on the blood of animals, mainly goats. It is reported in Latin America and parts of the United States.

Yeti (Abominable Snowman): A wild man-like creature said to inhabit the Himalayas and other mountainous regions.

Loch Ness Monster: A supposed aquatic creature believed to live in Loch Ness in Scotland.

Mothman: A winged figure with red eyes that is said to portend disasters. Seen in West Virginia, United States.

Jersey Devil: A being with wings and horns, it is said to live in the forests of New Jersey, United States.

The Wendigo: Mythological creature from the Algonquian tradition, often represented as a cannibalistic being with human appearance.

The Mokele-Snake: A dinosaur-like aquatic creature, supposedly sighted in African rivers.

The Mapinguari: An ape-like creature with only one eye and a mouth on its abdomen, according to Amazonian mythology.

The Kappa: An aquatic being from Japanese mythology, often described as a frogman.

El Yowie: A Bigfoot-like creature reported in Australia.

The Thunderbird: A giant bird from Native American legends, often associated with thunder and lightning.

The Chaneque: Mythological creature from Mexican tradition, known for playing pranks and pranks.

The Bunyip: An aquatic creature from Australian Aboriginal mythology.

El Mamlambo: An aquatic being with the appearance of a snake, according to Zulu mythology.

El Alux: Mythological creature from Mayan tradition, often associated with the protection of nature.

El Mawas: An ape-like creature reported in Malaysia.

The Hopkinsville Goblin: Small humanoid creatures reported in Kentucky, United States.

The Ahool: A giant bat reported in Java, Indonesia.

The Loveland Frogman: A toad-like creature, supposedly seen in Ohio, United States.

The Mantis Man: A humanoid figure with praying mantis characteristics, reported in different places.

El Flatwood's Monster: Humanoid-shaped creature with glowing eyes, reported in West Virginia, United States.

He Nobody: Giant sea creature reported in Antarctic waters.

El Kraken: A legendary marine creature, often depicted as a giant octopus.

ENIGMA OF THE UNKNOWN: WHAT ARE AND WHAT ARE NOT CRYPTIDS?

In the vast realm of the unknown, where shadows give shape to myths and legends, the enigmatic figure of the cryptids arises. But what exactly defines these beings and what distinguishes them from fantastic creatures and other manifestations of the human imagination? This chapter seeks to clarify the boundaries between reality and fantasy, exploring the essential characteristics that make a creature a cryptid and differentiating them from their fantastical counterparts.

What Are Cryptids?

Cryptids are creatures that defy conventional classification, whether due to their elusive nature, their lack of conclusive evidence, or their existence on the peripheries of human knowledge. These creatures, often considered myths or urban legends, have captured the imagination of generations, giving rise to tales of close encounters, mysterious sightings, and folklore narratives.

Key Characteristics of Cryptids:

1. Elusiveness: Cryptids tend to be elusive and difficult to capture or study. Their ability to evade direct detection contributes to the mystery surrounding them.

2. Lack of Solid Evidence: Although there are numerous accounts and testimonies, concrete physical evidence of the existence of cryptids is often elusive. Footprints, photographs and videos may be questionable in their authenticity.

3. Roots in Oral and Popular Tradition: Many cryptids have their roots in oral and popular tradition, being transmitted over time through local stories and folklore.

What Are Not Cryptids?

As we explore the boundaries of the mysterious, it is crucial to distinguish between cryptids and creatures that originate in fantasy, mythology, or fiction. Here, we highlight some categories that, while fascinating, do not fall within the realm of cryptids.

Fantastic Creatures

Dragons, Unicorns and Mythical Beings: These creatures, often present in mythology and fairy tales, are considered fantastic entities and not physical beings that can inhabit our world.

Paranormal Beings

Ghosts, Demons and Supernatural Entities: Although these

manifestations may be the subject of personal experiences and cultural beliefs, they do not fit the concept of cryptids, since their existence is beyond natural laws.

Creatures Created by Fiction

Monsters from Movies and Literature: Characters like Godzilla or the Swamp Monster, while intriguing and entertaining, are products of the imagination and are not considered cryptids in the traditional sense.

At the intersection of the tangible and the enigmatic, cryptids awaken our fascination with the unknown. As we continue on this journey, it is essential to cautiously approach the boundaries between reality and fantasy, exploring narratives critically and keeping an open mind to the wonders the world may still have in store. In the following chapters, we will delve deeper into the realm of these elusive creatures, questioning, exploring and unraveling the mysteries that have endured throughout time.

FACT OR MYTH?

Supporters of the existence of cryptids offer various explanations and theories to support their belief in these mysterious creatures. Although it is important to note that these explanations do not always have scientific support, they reflect the fascination and curiosity surrounding cryptids. Here are some of the most common explanations given by supporters:

Unknown Species: Some believe that cryptids could be animal species not identified by science. They maintain that in remote and little-explored areas of the world, creatures that have not yet been cataloged and studied could exist.

Survival of Extinct Species: It is suggested that certain cryptids could be species that were believed to be extinct but that have managed to survive in isolated regions. This theory is often associated with creatures such as the Mokele-Mbembe, linked to the idea of a dinosaur that still persists in certain places.

Extreme Adaptation: Some argue that cryptids are extremely adapted life forms evolved to survive in specific environments, which would explain why they are so difficult to detect and study.

Unknown Dimensions: A more speculative theory suggests that cryptids could come from alternate or parallel dimensions. According to this perspective, these creatures could cross between realities, appearing sporadically in our world.

Nature's Hypersensitivity: Some maintain that certain cryptids possess abilities that allow them to easily evade human detection, such as a form of natural camouflage or an ability to avoid tracking technology.

Mythology and Cultural Tradition: In some cases, supporters of the existence of cryptids argue that these creatures have roots in mythology and cultural tradition, which supports their existence throughout history and suggests that they could have real foundations.

The scientific community and cryptids

The predominant position among the scientific community is skepticism regarding the existence of cryptids. Scientists typically take a stance based on empirical evidence and scientific methodology, and to date, there is no conclusive evidence to support the existence of these mysterious creatures. Below are some of the main reasons why scientists tend to dismiss the existence of cryptids:

Lack of Compelling Evidence: Despite numerous reports and sightings, the lack of solid, verifiable physical evidence has been a significant obstacle. Blurred photographs, dubious videos, and controversial footprints have not provided conclusive evidence of the existence of cryptids.

Absence of Documented Species: Scientists argue that, given the current state of biological knowledge, it would be unlikely that unknown large mammals or reptiles would exist in widely explored and inhabited areas.

Challenge to the Principles of Biology and Ecology: Some of the cryptid descriptions defy basic principles of biology and ecology. For example, creatures that resemble living dinosaurs (such as the Mokele-Mbembe) contradict current understanding of Earth's evolutionary history.

Evolutionary Pressure and Environmental Change: Scientists maintain that, in the absence of solid evidence, the most likely explanation for the lack of detection of certain creatures is that they simply do not exist. Furthermore, they argue that if there were significant populations of these beings, evolutionary pressure and environmental change would make it difficult to continuously hide their presence.

Alternative Explanations: Many cryptid sightings can be explained by natural phenomena, misunderstandings of observations of common animals, or even fraud and hoaxes. Science tends to look for simpler, evidence-backed explanations before accepting more extraordinary

MAGNUS OLIVIER

hypotheses.

FROM LEGEND TO REALITY: CRYPTIDS DISCOVERED

Throughout history, numerous legends and myths have revolved around the existence of mysterious creatures. However, in certain cases, the line between fantasy and reality has been blurred when it has been discovered that some of these creatures, considered cryptids, were real. This chapter delves into the fascinating stories of creatures that were once classified as enigmas but were eventually revealed to be genuine.

The Discovery of the Okapi:

Historical context:

In the late 19th century, accounts from European explorers and missionaries in central Africa told of a strange creature that resembled a horse but with striped legs, a long neck, and a prehensile tongue. The reports were so incredible that many considered the animal, known as the Okapi, to be something of an African legend.

Discovery and Confirmation:

In 1901, naturalist Sir Harry Johnston managed to obtain Okapi skins and bones, confirming the existence of this creature in the Congo jungle. The Okapi turned out to be a close relative of the giraffe, with unique characteristics that allow it to move undetected in the dense jungle foliage.

The Gorilla Case:

Historical context:

Although gorillas were known to local populations in Africa, descriptions of these large and powerful creatures reached Europe in the 19th century through reports from explorers. Gorillas were initially considered mythological beings or exaggerations of stories.

Discovery and Confirmation:

It was only in 1847 that naturalist Thomas Savage obtained gorilla bones and skulls, proving that these creatures were real. Since then, gorillas have been studied extensively, and their existence is no longer an enigma.

The Coelacanth: A Living Fossil:

Historical context:

The Coelacanth was known only through fossils and was believed to have become extinct millions of years ago. However, in 1938, a South African fisherman captured a live specimen of this species, challenging the scientific beliefs of the time.

Discovery and Confirmation:

The living Coelacanth was described by ichthyologist Marjorie Courtenay-Latimer. This shocking discovery demonstrated that a species previously considered extinct continued to exist in the deep ocean.

These cases highlight how reality is sometimes stranger than fiction and how creatures once considered cryptids have been revealed as a tangible part of our planet's biodiversity. Although many cryptids are still awaiting their moment of confirmation, these examples serve as a reminder that, in the vastness of nature, there is still much to discover and understand. In the coming chapters, we will explore the unsolved puzzles and surprises that nature may still have in store for us.

BIGFOOT

The legend of Bigfoot, also known as Sasquatch, is one of the most famous and enduring in North American folk mythology. This mysterious being is described as a large ape-like creature that would inhabit remote, forested areas of North America, especially in regions such as the Pacific Northwest and the Rocky Mountains. The figure of Bigfoot has captured the imagination of countless people over the years, sparking speculation, sightings and debates about its existence.

Anatomy and Personality Revealed

The figure of Bigfoot is characterized by its simian appearance and its large stature, generally between 7 and 10 feet tall. It is described as a primate covered in hair, with humanoid features but with more animalistic characteristics, such as large feet and ape-like hands. Although details vary according to reports, it is generally depicted as a robust, muscular creature, with a large head and expressive eyes. It is often credited with an upright posture, similar to that of humans.

As for his character, descriptions vary. Some legends present it as a peaceful and timid creature, while others suggest more aggressive behavior, especially if it feels threatened. Bigfoot is believed to be primarily nocturnal and moves stealthily through forests, contributing to its elusive nature.

Exploring your Remote Habitat

Typical Bigfoot habitat is forested and remote, with densely forested and mountainous areas providing cover and isolation. Regions such as the Gifford Pinchot National Forest in Washington and the Six Rivers National Forest in California are known for sightings of this creature. The idea that Bigfoot can live in such vast, hard-to-reach areas has contributed to the difficulty of obtaining conclusive evidence of its existence.

Memorable Encounters

Over the years, there have been numerous reports of Bigfoot sightings in various regions of North America. From the infamous Patterson-Gimlin film to the incidents at Ape Canyon, explore the most notorious encounters that have fueled the ongoing narrative of this elusive creature.

1. The Patterson-Gimlin Sighting (1967): This is one of the most famous and controversial sightings. Filmmakers Roger Patterson and Bob Gimlin claimed to have filmed a female Bigfoot in Bluff Creek, California. The footage, known as the "Patterson-Gimlin film," shows a creature walking upright across a clearing.

2. The Ape Canyon Incident (1924): A group of miners claimed to have been attacked by a group of Bigfoots in the Ape Canyon area of Mount St. Helens, Washington. Stones were reported thrown towards his cabin, leading to

a violent confrontation.

3. The Sighting of Albert Ostman (1924): Ostman claimed to have been abducted by a Bigfoot while camping in the Toba Mountains of British Columbia, during which he shared a cave with the creature for several days before escaping.

4. The Ruby Creek Sighting (1941): A group of construction workers reported seeing a Bigfoot near Ruby Creek, British Columbia, Canada.

These sightings, along with many other anecdotal reports, have fueled the ongoing narrative of Bigfoot as a real creature roaming the forests of North America.

Between Science and Speculation

The scientific community generally does not support the existence of Bigfoot due to a lack of conclusive evidence. Although numerous expeditions and searches have been carried out to find evidence, such as footprints and DNA samples, no solid, verifiable evidence has been found so far.

Theories regarding the existence of Bigfoot vary. Some believe it could be an unidentified species of primate, possibly a relative of the extinct primate gigantopithecus. Others suggest that the sightings are simply misinterpretations of bears, men dressed in ape suits, or other natural phenomena.

The lack of conclusive physical evidence has led many

to consider the possibility that Bigfoot is more of a mythological or cultural figure than an actual biological creature. Some suggest that the legend of Bigfoot may have roots in indigenous myths and oral traditions, which have been reinterpreted and adapted over time.

5 Curiosities about Bigfoot:

1. Varied Name: The term "Bigfoot" was popularized in the 1950s, but different cultures and regions have different names for this creature. In Native American mythology, he is known by various names, such as Sasquatch, Skookum, or simply Hairy Man.

2. Tracking Footprints: One of the elements most cited as evidence of the existence of Bigfoot are the footprints found in the forests. However, the authenticity of many of these footprints has been questioned, as they can be easily replicated or attributed to other animal species.

3. Pop Culture: Bigfoot has left his mark on popular culture, appearing in numerous movies, television shows, and books. It is a recurring theme in science fiction, comedy and mystery documentaries.

4. International Bigfoot Day: In honor of this legendary creature,

September 30 marks International Bigfoot Day, an occasion to reflect on the legend and its impact on popular culture.

5. Rewards for Evidence: Over the years, considerable rewards have been offered for conclusive evidence of the existence of Bigfoot. However, none of these offerings have been claimed, adding more mystery to the legend.

THE LEGEND OF THE CHUPACABRA

The legend of the Chupacabra is a narrative that has permeated the nights of Latin America and, to a lesser extent, other parts of the world. This mysterious being is known for its supposed predilection for the blood of animals, primarily goats, which has sparked speculation, fear, and numerous accounts of terrifying encounters.

Physical and Character Description:

The Chupacabra is described in various ways, but is commonly depicted as a medium-sized being, with a reptilian or alien appearance. It usually has large red eyes, sharp claws, and is, in some reports, winged. The creature is associated with attacks on barnyard animals, especially sucking the blood of goats and other livestock. Although descriptions vary, the figure of the Chupacabra usually evokes fear and is considered a threat to livestock.

Place of Appearance:

Sightings of the Chupacabra have been reported primarily in Latin America, although reports have also been recorded in the United States and elsewhere. Countries such as Puerto Rico, Mexico and others in Central and South

America have been the scene of numerous stories about encounters with this creature.

Main Sightings:

1. Initial Incidents in Puerto Rico (1995): The Chupacabra first gained notoriety in Puerto Rico in 1995, when a series of attacks on barnyard animals were reported. Witnesses described a reptile-like creature with spines on its back and a long tongue used to suck blood.

2. Surge of Sightings in Mexico (2000): In the early 2000s, Mexico experienced a surge of reports of Chupacabras. The creature was claimed to attack animals and leave characteristic marks, such as small puncture holes, on the victims' bodies.

3. Alleged Capture in Texas (2004): In 2004, the capture of a creature thought to be a Chupacabra was reported in Texas. However, the identity of the captured animal was disputed, with some arguing that it was simply a coyote with mange.

These are just a few examples of the numerous sightings that have fueled the Chupacabra legend.

Opinions and Theories:

The scientific community generally considers the Chupacabra legend to be a combination of myths, erroneous explanations, and natural phenomena. In many cases, animals attacked by the Chupacabra have turned out to be victims of common predators or diseases. The absence of conclusive evidence has led to the conclusion that the creature is more of a cultural and folkloric construction than a real biological entity.

5 Curiosities about the Chupacabra:

1. Origins in Puerto Rico: Although the Chupacabra has become part of Latin American mythology, its first reports emerged in Puerto Rico in the 1990s.

2. Variety of Descriptions: Over the years, descriptions of the Chupacabra have varied significantly, from a reptilian being to more dog-like creatures.

3. Extended Mythology: As the legend of the Chupacabra spread, additional myths were generated about its ability to hypnotize its victims or change shape.

4. Impact on Pop Culture: The Chupacabra has left its mark on popular culture, appearing in television shows, movies and literature, often as a fearsome and monstrous being.

5. Chupacabra Hunters: Some people have claimed to be "Chupacabra hunters", organizing expeditions to search for evidence of the existence of this creature. However, so far, no conclusive evidence has been presented.

THE LEGEND OF THE YETI

The legend of the Yeti, also known as the "Abominable Snowman," has fascinated explorers and adventurers for centuries. This mysterious being is supposedly an ape-like creature that inhabits the mountainous regions of the Himalayas, capturing the public's imagination with its enigma and the possibility of an as yet unknown primate species.

Physical and Character Description:

The Yeti is generally described as a large, hairy creature, similar to an ape or a wild man. Their fur varies in shades, from white to dark brown, adapting to their mountainous environment. The Yeti is believed to be bipedal, walking upright, and possessing humanoid features such as clawed hands and a round head with expressive eyes. Unlike other legendary creatures, the Yeti is not commonly associated with aggressive behavior towards humans in narratives.

Place of Appearance:

The Yeti is mainly linked to the Himalayan mountain ranges, which run through Nepal, Tibet, Bhutan and India. Local populations have shared stories about the Yeti for generations, attributing encounters and sightings to these vast, remote mountain regions.

Main Sightings:

1. Traditional Encounters in the Himalayas: Local communities have passed down stories of encounters with the Yeti for centuries. These accounts vary from simple sightings to closer encounters, but in general, the creature is perceived as an elusive figure that easily eludes human detection.

2. The Expedition of Colonel Howard-Bury (1921): During an expedition to Mount Everest, Colonel Charles Howard-Bury and his team discovered footprints in the snow that they attributed to the Yeti. This event was one of the first to bring the legend of the Yeti to Western attention.

3. The Eric Shipton Incident (1951): During another expedition to Everest, explorer Eric Shipton photographed footprints that he believed belonged to the Yeti. The images, known as the "Shipton footprints," contributed to the popularity of the myth.

Opinions and Theories:

Claims about the Yeti are generally considered by science to be most likely attributable to natural phenomena, cultural misunderstandings, or sightings of local animals. The footprints attributed to the Yeti are often explained as tracks left by animals such as bears, and some accounts may derive from encounters with unidentified primates or even from human imagination itself.

Despite the lack of conclusive scientific evidence, the Yeti myth persists as an integral part of Himalayan culture and has attracted global attention.

5 Curiosities About the Yeti:

1. The "Myth of the Wild Man": The figure of the Yeti is often associated with the "myth of the wild man" present in various cultures, which suggests the existence of humanoid beings that live apart from society.

2. Comparison to Bigfoot: Although the Yeti and Bigfoot share similarities in their physical description, they are associated with different geographic regions: the Yeti in the Himalayas and the Bigfoot in North America.

3. Yeh-teh or Meh-teh: In local traditions, the Yeti is known by different names, such as "Yeh-teh" in Nepal and "Meh-teh" in Tibet.

4. Modern Explorations: Despite the lack of solid evidence, modern expeditions continue in search of the Yeti, using advanced technology such as drones and high-resolution cameras to document possible encounters.

5. Footprint of the Yeti: In 2011, the Nepalese government introduced a set of rules to regulate expeditions in search of the Yeti, including a ban on destroying or damaging any evidence that might belong to the creature.

THE LEGEND OF THE LOCH NESS MONSTER

The legend of the Loch Ness Monster has intrigued humanity for decades, turning the dark waters of the lake into a mysterious setting full of speculation and controversial sightings. The creature, affectionately known as Nessie, has captured the public's imagination and has become an iconic symbol of cryptozoology.

Physical and Character Description:

The Loch Ness Monster is commonly described as a large aquatic creature with a long neck and a head that occasionally emerges from the dark waters of the lake. Nessie has been depicted in a variety of ways, from a giant snake to a prehistoric plesiosaur, but the most common description is a plesiosaur-like animal with a long neck.

Place of Appearance:

The Loch Ness Monster is primarily associated with Loch Ness in the Scottish Highlands. With its deep darkness and mysterious waters, the lake has become the epicenter of the search for Nessie, attracting visitors and explorers alike.

Main Sightings:

1. The Sighting of 1933: The sighting that catapulted the legend of the Loch Ness Monster occurred in 1933, when a couple claimed to have seen a creature with a long neck crossing the road that borders the lake.

2. The Photograph of 1934 (The famous photo of the Loch Ness Monster emerges): In 1934, the surgeon R.K. Wilson captured a famous photograph showing what appeared to be Nessie's neck and head emerging from the water. Although this image has been highly debated and is considered a fraud by some, it contributed significantly to the popularity of the myth.

3. 2011 Sonar: In 2011, a team of researchers used sonar technology to scan Loch Ness, claiming to have detected a large, moving object about 180 meters deep. However, the interpretation of these results remains debated.

Opinions and Theories:

Science generally dismisses the existence of a large prehistoric monster in Loch Ness due to a lack of conclusive evidence. The most widely accepted theories suggest that the sightings could be explained by natural phenomena, such as floating logs, optical illusions or even real animals that may appear extraordinary from certain perspectives.

5 Curiosities about the Loch Ness Monster:

1. Nessie in Popular Culture: Nessie has become a symbol

of Scotland and has left her mark on popular culture, appearing in films, books and television shows.

2. More Photos and Videos: Over the years, numerous photos and videos purporting to show Nessie have been captured, but many of them have been debunked or questioned.

3. Rewards for Evidence: As with other cryptids, rewards have been offered for conclusive evidence of the existence of the Loch Ness Monster, but none have been claimed.

4. The Loch Ness Project: In 2018, the Loch Ness Project team conducted an extensive genetic study of the lake water to analyze DNA and look for possible traces of unusual life, although the results did not confirm the presence of large unknown creatures. .

5. Nessie Monument: In Drumnadrochit, on the shores of the lake, is the Loch Ness Monster Exhibition Centre, which houses a monument dedicated to Nessie and tells the story of the legend.

THE LEGEND OF MOTHMAN

The legend of the Mothman has captivated those interested in the paranormal and the unknown. This creature, described as a winged figure with glowing red eyes, has been linked to mysterious events and tragedies, sparking speculation and conspiracy theories.

Physical and Character Description:

Mothman is commonly described as a winged creature, of great stature and glowing red eyes. Its appearance resembles that of a giant moth or a winged man. The wings, which spread considerably, are a distinctive feature. Its presence is often associated with feelings of unease or premonitions of impending disaster.

Place of Appearance:

The legend of the Mothman is mainly linked to the city of Point Pleasant, West Virginia, United States. The creature was reported in the 1960s, especially before the tragic collapse of the Point Pleasant Silver Bridge in 1967, which has led to some interpretations of the Mothman as a harbinger of disaster.

Main Sightings:

1. Point Pleasant Sightings Series (1966): Several people reported encounters with the Mothman in the months leading up to the collapse of the Silver Bridge. Some witnesses described the feeling of unease before the disaster.

2. The Silver Bridge Collapse (1967): On December 15, 1967, the Point Pleasant Silver Bridge collapsed, causing loss of life. After the incident, Mothman sightings decreased, contributing to speculation about his connection to the disaster.

Opinions and Theories:

The interpretation of Mothman varies. Some believe it is a paranormal or even extraterrestrial creature, while others see it as a supernatural entity associated with catastrophic events. Science and skepticism often dismiss Mothman as a combination of misunderstanding, common animal sightings, and collective suggestion.

5 Fun Facts about Mothman:

1. "The Mothman Prophecies" Book: The Mothman legend was further popularized by the book "The Mothman Prophecies" by John Keel, which examines the events at Point Pleasant and speculates on paranormal connections.

2. Film and Adaptations: The Mothman story has inspired several films, including "The Mothman Prophecies" released in 2002, starring Richard Gere.

3. Mothman Statue: In Point Pleasant, a Mothman statue is erected in town as a tribute to the legend. The city also hosts an annual festival dedicated to the Mothman.

4. Extraterrestrial Theories: Some theories suggest that Mothman could be a creature of extraterrestrial origin, and his appearance in places with tragic events could be due to his ability to foresee disasters.

5. Red Eyes as Omen: In many sighting stories, the Mothman's red eyes are associated with premonitions of catastrophic events, adding a terrifying element to his legend.

THE LEGEND OF THE JERSEY DEVIL

The legend of the Jersey Devil, also known as the "Jersey Devil," is one of America's most notorious cryptozoologies. This creature, with an appearance that mixes characteristics of various animals, has been an integral part of New Jersey folklore for centuries, generating fear and speculation about its origin.

Physical and Character Description:

The Jersey Devil is commonly described as a creature with features that include a horse-like head, membranous wings, crane-like hind legs, and a long, serpentine tail. Its grotesque appearance and ability to fly distinguish it from similar creatures in mythology. It is believed to emit a piercing screech, which contributes to its terrifying aura.

Place of Appearance:

The legend of the Jersey Devil is closely linked to the forests and wildernesses of the state of New Jersey, United States. The creature is believed to lurk in these rural and wooded areas, stalking those who venture too close to its supposed habitat.

Main Sightings:

1. 18th Century Origins: The legend of the Jersey Devil dates back to the 18th century, with stories suggesting that the creature is the result of a curse placed by Mother Leeds, a local woman.

2. Sightings in the 19th Century: During the 19th century, numerous sightings of the Jersey Devil were reported in New Jersey and surrounding areas. These sightings were often linked to the creature's presence on stormy nights.

3. Most Recent Incidents: Over the years, there have been sporadic reports of sightings of the Jersey Devil, although none have provided conclusive evidence of its existence.

Opinions and Theories:

The legend of the Jersey Devil has largely been considered myth and folklore. Although some sightings have been reported, the lack of solid physical evidence has led most researchers to rule out the creature's actual existence. It is suggested that the sightings could be attributable to wild animals, such as owls or foxes, misunderstandings or even natural phenomena.

5 Curiosities about the Jersey Devil:

1. The Curse of Mother Leeds: According to legend, the Jersey Devil was the result of the curse pronounced by Mother Leeds, a local woman who, tired of having children, wished that her next child would be the devil.

2. New Jersey Pine Country: Most Jersey Devil sightings focus on the New Jersey Pine Country, a vast forested area known for its isolation and mystery.

3. Frightening Screech: The Jersey Devil is said to make a terrifying screech, which has contributed to its reputation as a fearsome creature.

4. Jersey Devil Festival: In the city of Leeds Point, New Jersey, the "Jersey Devil Festival" is held annually, an occasion to commemorate the legend with themed events and activities.

5. Appearances in Popular Culture: The Jersey Devil has left his mark on popular culture, appearing in films, books and television shows, contributing to his persistence as a mythical figure.

THE LEGEND OF THE WENDIGO

The legend of the Wendigo is a narrative rooted in the traditions of the indigenous peoples of North America, especially among the Algonquian communities. The Wendigo is an evil, spiritual creature, associated with extreme hunger and greed, that has captured the imagination and fear of generations.

Physical and Character Description:

The Wendigo is described in various ways, but is commonly depicted as a emaciated, skeletal figure, with its skin stretched over its bones. It often has sunken eyes and sharp horns on its head. His appearance reflects his connection to hunger and despair. In addition to its physical appearance, the Wendigo is also linked to spirit possession and cannibalism.

Place of Appearance:

The legend of the Wendigo has its roots in the remote, forested regions of the northern United States and Canada, where Algonquian communities have shared stories about this creature. The Wendigo is believed to lurk in the forests during harsh winters and times of famine, seeking out those who have fallen into despair and greed.

Main Cultural Aspects:

1. Cannibalism and Spiritual Corruption: The figure of the Wendigo is intrinsically linked to the act of cannibalism and the spiritual corruption that results from that action. It is said that those who resort to cannibalism, especially in situations of extreme hunger, risk becoming Wendigos.

2. Hunger and Despair: The Wendigo emerges in times of extreme famine, when communities face difficult conditions to find food. The legend warns of the dangers of greed and the loss of humanity in the midst of despair.

Opinions and Theories:

The legend of the Wendigo is primarily cultural and spiritual, rooted in the beliefs and traditions of indigenous peoples. The figure of the Wendigo is not considered a real physical entity by conventional science, but rather as a myth that transmits teachings about the importance of moderation, solidarity and respect for nature.

5 Curiosities about the Wendigo:

1. Representation in Literature: The legend of the Wendigo has inspired numerous literary works, including the short story "The Wendigo" by Algernon Blackwood and the novel "Pet Sematary" by Stephen King.

2. Warning Symbol: The figure of the Wendigo serves as a spiritual warning against greed and cannibalism, reminding communities of the importance of maintaining

a balance with nature.

3. Variants in Stories: Although the essence of the Wendigo is consistent across many traditions, there are variations in stories and depictions depending on specific indigenous communities.

4. Transformation in Pop Culture: Over time, the Wendigo has found its place in popular culture, appearing in films, television series and video games, although often in a different way from its original representation.

5. Cultural Celebration: Some indigenous communities hold ceremonies and events to honor the Wendigo tradition and remember the lessons it offers about ethics and social responsibility.

THE LEGEND OF THE MOKELE-MBEMBE

The Mokele-Mbembe is a legendary creature that is part of the mythology of some African communities, especially in the Congo region. This creature has been described as a large aquatic animal, often compared to a prehistoric sauropod, such as a dinosaur. The legend of the Mokele-Mbembe has sparked interest and speculation in the cryptozoology community.

Physical and Character Description:

The Mokele-Mbembe is described as an aquatic creature with a long neck and a head that resembles that of a dinosaur. Its size is commonly compared to that of an elephant or larger. This creature is believed to inhabit rivers and lakes, staying in deep waters and hiding in remote and hard-to-access areas.

Place of Appearance:

The legend of the Mokele-Mbembe is mainly associated with the jungles and bodies of water in the Congo region, especially in the Congo River basin. The creature is believed to reside in unexplored and hard-to-reach areas, which has contributed to the lack of concrete evidence for its existence.

Main Sightings:

1. Local Stories: Stories about the Mokele-Mbembe have been passed down through generations in local communities. The creature is said to be shy and avoids contact with humans.

2. Explorations and Expeditions: Over the years, there have been expeditions and research trips aimed at finding evidence of the Mokele-Mbembe. However, to date, there has been no conclusive evidence of the existence of this creature.

Opinions and Theories:

The scientific community has been skeptical about the existence of the Mokele-Mbembe due to a lack of tangible evidence. It has been suggested that descriptions of the creature could coincide with sightings of known animals, such as elephants, hippos or crocodiles, but interpreted in a mythological or exaggerated way.

Some cryptozoology enthusiasts believe that the Mokele-Mbembe could be a surviving species of dinosaur, while others consider it more likely to be an unknown creature of biological origin. However, the lack of solid physical evidence has kept the legend in the realm of speculation.

5 Curiosities about the Mokele-Mbembe:

1. Cultural Influence: The legend of the Mokele-Mbembe has influenced local culture, and his image often appears

on artifacts and cultural representations of the region.

2. Parallels with Dinosaurs: Descriptions of the Mokele-Mbembe often resemble dinosaurs, which has led to comparisons with prehistoric creatures.

3. Controversial Explorations: Some expeditions to find the Mokele-Mbembe have been the subject of controversy and criticism due to the lack of conclusive results.

4. Documentaries and Reports: The legend has been the subject of documentaries and reports that explore the possibility of its existence, generating interest in cryptozoology.

5. Local Mythology: In addition to being considered a physical creature, the Mokele-Mbembe is also an integral part of local mythology and beliefs, with stories that convey lessons and symbolic meanings.

THE LEGEND OF THE MAPINGUARI

The Mapinguari is a legendary creature that is part of the folklore of the Amazon regions of Brazil and other South American countries. This creature has been described in various ways, but is commonly depicted as a large, hairy being, with characteristics that generate fear and speculation in local communities.

Physical and Character Description:

The appearance of the Mapinguari varies in descriptions, but it is commonly represented as a large, hairy being, with characteristics that resemble an ape or a werebeast. Some versions describe the Mapinguari with a mouth on its abdomen and feet facing backwards, while others depict it with only one leg and a mouth on its navel. It is said to emit a strong odor and have supernatural abilities.

Place of Appearance:

The legends of the Mapinguari come from the jungles and forests of the Amazon region, where the creature is said to live. Their presence has been reported in remote and difficult-to-access areas, contributing to the mysterious nature of the legend.

Main Sightings:

1. Oral Stories: The existence of the Mapinguari is transmitted mainly through oral stories and legends transmitted from generation to generation in the Amazonian indigenous communities.

2. Contemporary Encounters: Over the years, there have been reports of contemporary encounters with the Mapinguari. However, these reports often lack conclusive evidence and are subject to skepticism.

Opinions and Theories:

The legend of the Mapinguari has sparked interest in the cryptozoology community, although most scientists and experts consider the creature to be more of a cultural myth than a real biological entity. Some theories suggest that the sightings may be attributed to misunderstandings with animals known from the region, such as anteaters or primates.

The legend of the Mapinguari may also have roots in mythology and indigenous beliefs, where the creature may have symbolic or spiritual meaning beyond its physical representation.

5 Curiosities about the Mapinguari:

1. Strong Smell: The Mapinguari is said to emit a strong and unpleasant odor, which is often mentioned in accounts of encounters.

2. Supernatural Abilities: Some versions of the legend attribute supernatural abilities to the Mapinguari, such as the ability to become invisible or to attract people to him.

3. Connection with Nature: In some interpretations, the Mapinguari is considered a protector of nature or a spirit linked to the biodiversity of the Amazon rainforest.

4. Regional Variations: The characteristics and description of the Mapinguari may vary depending on the region and community that shares the legend, which adds complexity to the narrative.

5. Impact on Local Culture: The legend of Mapinguari has left its mark on local culture, influencing the worldview and traditions of Amazonian communities.

THE LEGEND OF KAPPA

The Kappa is a legendary creature from Japanese mythology, known for inhabiting bodies of water, such as rivers and ponds. Although he has several representations in different tales and legends, he is usually described as a turtle-like being with humanoid characteristics, and is often both a feared and respected figure in Japanese folklore tradition.

Physical and Character Description:

The Kappa is generally depicted as a reptilian-like creature, with a shell on its back similar to that of a turtle. It has a concave head that retains water, considered vital for its existence. Its skin is green and slippery, and its limbs are webbed. One of the Kappa's most distinctive features is a depression on the top of its head, which it must keep filled with water to conserve its strength and energy.

Although the Kappa can be malicious, it is also credited with the ability to show gratitude, and is said to respect those who return its greeting by bowing, which causes the water contained in its head to spill out and momentarily weakens it.

Place of Appearance:

Stories of the Kappa are common throughout Japan and have been part of Japanese mythology for centuries. These creatures are believed to inhabit bodies of fresh water, such as rivers, ponds, and lakes.

Main Cultural Characteristics:

1. Mischief and Playfulness: The Kappa is known for being mischievous and sometimes playful. It can be a threat to humans, especially children, but it is also said to have fun competing in sumo games or throwing watermelon seeds.

2. The Shiryō: It is believed that the Kappa possesses a "shiryō" (or soul) in its head. By losing water from your head, you become weaker and can be less dangerous.

Opinions and Theories:

The figure of the Kappa is mainly considered a mythological and folkloric creature in Japanese culture. Although belief in the Kappa has waned over time, it remains a popular figure in cultural tradition and artistic representations.

5 Curiosities about Kappa:

1. Bowing Greeting: The Kappa is said to respond to a greeting by bowing, causing water to spill from its head. Encounters with a Kappa can be peaceful if this protocol is followed.

2. Favorite Foods: The Kappa is believed to enjoy cucumbers

and, in some legends, the cucumber is used as an offering to appease these aquatic creatures.

3. Kawa-no-kami: In some regions of Japan, Kappa is worshiped as "kawa-no-kami" or "river god." Rituals are performed to appease these creatures and ensure safety in the water.

4. The Kappa and Children: Stories of the Kappa are often used as a warning for children to be careful when playing near bodies of water, promoting safety and caution.

5. Representation in Popular Culture: Kappa has left its mark on Japanese popular culture, appearing in numerous books, films and television shows. His image has also been used on toys and traditional items.

THE LEGEND OF THE YOWIE:

The Yowie is a legendary creature that is part of Aboriginal folklore in Australia, specifically among indigenous communities. This creature is described as a species of large hominid or ape that lives in the forested and remote areas of the continent. The legend of the Yowie has persisted over time, generating speculation and unconfirmed sightings in Australian culture.

Physical and Character Description:

The physical description of the Yowie varies in different accounts, but it is commonly depicted as an ape- or hominid-like creature, large in size and covered in hair. Some descriptions suggest that it has human features, such as hands and feet similar to those of people, but with a more primitive and wild appearance. Its fur can be dark and thick, adapting to the wooded environment in which it is said to reside.

In terms of character, the Yowie is often presented as a shy and elusive creature, avoiding contact with humans. However, more aggressive behavior is also attributed to it if it feels threatened.

Place of Appearance:

Yowie stories come from various regions of Australia, especially in forested and remote areas. The Yowie is believed to inhabit natural environments and avoid human presence as much as possible.

Main Sightings:

Over the years, there have been numerous reports and unconfirmed sightings of the Yowie in different parts of Australia. These reports often come from people claiming to have seen a large, hairy creature in remote areas, but the lack of solid physical evidence has led to widespread skepticism.

Opinions and Theories:

The scientific community generally does not support the existence of the Yowie due to a lack of conclusive evidence. Although some researchers and cryptozoology enthusiasts have conducted searches and expeditions in search of evidence, no definitive trace of the creature has been found so far.

Some theories suggest that the Yowie sightings could be misinterpretations of animals native to Australia, such as kangaroos or emus, or even natural phenomena. The legend of the Yowie may also have roots in oral traditions and indigenous myths, which have been reinterpreted over time.

5 Curiosities about the Yowie:

1. Regional Names: Although the term "Yowie" is widely used, different regions of Australia have local names for similar creatures. Some of these include "Quinkin" and "Jingera."

2. Presence in Aboriginal Myths: The figure of the Yowie has parallels with creatures present in myths and legends of Aboriginal communities in Australia. Their presence is often part of the rich oral tradition of these cultures.

3. Frequent Sighting Regions: Reports of sightings of the Yowie often come from areas such as the Queensland rainforest and the Blue Mountains in New South Wales.

4. Comparisons with Other Cryptids: The Yowie is sometimes compared to other similar creatures from different parts of the world, such as the Bigfoot in North America or the Yeti in the Himalayas.

5. Appearances in Popular Culture: The figure of the Yowie has inspired stories, films and performances in Australian popular culture, contributing to his place in the country's modern mythology.

THE LEGEND OF
THE THUNDERBIRD

The Thunderbird is a mythical creature that appears in the legends of various indigenous North American cultures, such as Native American tribes. This creature is considered a powerful and sacred being, associated with meteorological phenomena, especially storms and thunder. The image of the Thunderbird varies in different traditions, but its presence is common in the cultural narratives of indigenous tribes.

Physical and Character Description:

The physical representation of the Thunderbird can vary depending on the tribe's tradition, but it is usually described as a giant bird with resplendent feathers and expansive wings. In some legends, its wings are said to produce thunder and lightning when they beat, and its cry is associated with the roar of thunder. The Thunderbird is often considered a majestic and powerful creature, connected to spirituality and nature.

Place of Appearance:

Stories of the Thunderbird are common in the Great Plains and Rocky Mountain regions of North America, where various indigenous tribes have passed down these legends for generations. The figure of the Thunderbird may also be present in other indigenous cultures of North America.

Main Cultural Aspects:

1. Guardian Spirit: The Thunderbird is often considered a guardian and protective spirit in many indigenous traditions. Its connection with nature and the meteorological elements gives it sacred status.

2. Association with Storms: The presence of the Thunderbird in legends is closely linked to the arrival of thunderstorms. Thunder is believed to be the sound produced by the Thunderbird's wings.

Opinions and Theories:

Unlike other mythical creatures, the Thunderbird is not considered a tangible physical being in indigenous beliefs, but rather a powerful spirit and spiritual entity. The figure of the Thunderbird has a deep connection with spirituality and the relationship of tribes with nature.

From a cultural perspective, the Thunderbird remains a revered and respected figure in many indigenous communities, and its presence in legends remains significant today.

5 Curiosities about the Thunderbird:

1. Regional Variations: The image and interpretation of the Thunderbird can vary significantly between different indigenous tribes. Each community can have its own

version of the legend.

2. Artistic Representation: The figure of the Thunderbird is often depicted on artifacts, totems, and works of art from indigenous cultures, highlighting its importance in the iconography of these communities.

3. Cultural Celebration: In some tribes, ceremonies and rituals are performed to honor the Thunderbird, especially during significant events or to seek protection and blessings.

4. Religious Syncretism: In some regions, Thunderbird legends have been mixed with elements of other religions, resulting in unique forms of spirituality.

5. Influence on Toponymy: The figure of the Thunderbird has influenced the toponymy of certain areas, and there are places in North America that bear its name in recognition of its importance in indigenous traditions.

THE LEGEND OF CHANEQUE

The Chaneque is a mythical creature belonging to Mexican folklore, especially rooted in the indigenous traditions of various regions of the country. This figure is known for his mischievous nature and his connection with nature, being considered both a protector and a being that can play pranks and pranks on those who enter his territory. The legend of Chaneque reflects the rich cultural diversity of Mexico and the beliefs that have been transmitted through generations.

Physical and Character Description:

The appearance of the Chaneque can vary in different stories and regions, but it is commonly described as a small being, similar to a child or an old man, with characteristics that evoke the magical and supernatural. It may have humanoid aspects, but animal features are also attributed to it, such as pointed ears or goat legs. His ability to shapeshift allows him to adapt to his surroundings and go unnoticed.

Regarding its character, the Chaneque is known for its playful and sometimes malicious personality. It is often associated with the protection of nature and its inhabitants, but can punish those who damage the environmental balance or enter areas considered sacred.

Place of Appearance:

The legends of Chaneque are present in various regions of Mexico, especially in forested and mountainous areas. These creatures are believed to inhabit natural environments, such as forests and jungles, where they play an active role in local mythology.

Main Cultural Aspects:

1. Guardians of Nature: The Chaneque is considered a guardian of nature and its inhabitants, protecting forests and natural areas from harmful human intervention.

2. Link with the Supernatural: Although the Chaneque manifests itself in a playful manner, it is also attributed with supernatural abilities and the ability to cause disorientation to those who enter its territory.

Opinions and Theories:

The figure of Chaneque is rooted in the beliefs and mythologies of the indigenous communities of Mexico. Although the legend may vary in details, its presence in Mexican culture reflects the importance of connection with nature and respectful coexistence with the environment.

From a cultural perspective, the Chaneque is considered more of a spiritual and mythical being than a physical creature. His role as protector of nature reflects the importance of sustainability and respect for the environment in local traditions.

5 Curiosities about Chaneque:

1. Avoidance Strategies: The Chaneque is believed to use tactics such as shape-shifting or the ability to become invisible to avoid detection by those entering its territory.

2. Offerings and Respect: To avoid the interference of the Chaneque, some communities make offerings and rituals to show respect for its presence and guarantee harmony with nature.

3. Oral Stories: The stories of Chaneque have been transmitted mainly through oral traditions, being shared from generation to generation.

4. Relationship with Other Mythical Beings: In some legends, the Chaneque is associated with other mythical creatures from Mexican mythology, such as the Nahual and the Alux.

5. Regional Adaptation: As the legend of Chaneque has spread throughout various regions of Mexico, its representation and characteristics may vary depending on local interpretation and specific cultural influences.

THE LEGEND OF BUNYIP

The Bunyip is a mythical creature that is part of Aboriginal mythology in Australia, specifically in the traditions of the indigenous peoples who inhabit the regions of lakes, rivers and swamps. The figure of the Bunyip has been transmitted through oral histories and legends, and its description varies between different Aboriginal communities.

Physical and Character Description:

The appearance of the Bunyip varies in different accounts, but it is commonly described as an aquatic creature, similar to a monster or spirit that inhabits lakes, rivers and stagnant waters. Physical descriptions include features such as furry skin, horns, fins, and sharp fangs. Their size can also vary, from being relatively small to giant. Bunyip is often associated with the darkness and mystery of the waters.

In terms of character, the Bunyip is considered a fearsome and mysterious creature. It is credited with terrifying sounds and the ability to cause harm to those who venture too close to its habitat.

Place of Appearance:

The Bunyip legends come mainly from the lake and river areas in Australia, such as the southeast and southwest of the country. These aquatic creatures are believed to inhabit natural environments and are especially associated with places with deep, dark waters.

Main Cultural Aspects:

1. Spiritual Creature: The Bunyip is often considered a spiritual creature with meaning beyond its physical representation. Its presence is linked to the relationship of indigenous communities with nature and water.

2. Warning and Respect: The legends of the Bunyip also serve as a warning to those who venture near dangerous bodies of water. Respect for nature and caution are common themes in these stories.

Opinions and Theories:

The figure of the Bunyip is not considered as a tangible physical entity in Aboriginal beliefs, but rather as a spiritual and mythological creature. Although modern science does not support the existence of the Bunyip as a real biological being, its cultural importance and role in transmitting knowledge about nature are recognized.

5 Curiosities about Bunyip:

1. Variety of Descriptions: The diversity in descriptions of the Bunyip reflects the rich variety of Aboriginal traditions in Australia. Each community may have its own

interpretation of the creature.

2. Origins of the Name: The word "Bunyip" comes from the Wemba-Wemba Aboriginal language in southeastern Australia. Its exact meaning may vary, but it is commonly associated with mysterious creatures.

3. Adaptation Over Time: Over the years, Bunyip legends have evolved and adapted, often influenced by changes in Australian society and culture.

4. Artistic Representation: The Bunyip has been represented in various forms in Aboriginal art and Australian popular culture, contributing to its presence in the country's iconography.

5. Influence on Literature: The figure of the Bunyip has inspired literary works and stories in Australian literature, being a lasting presence in creativity and cultural expression.

THE LEGEND OF MAMLAMBO

The Mamlambo is a mythical creature that is part of Zulu mythology in South Africa. Described as an aquatic being, the Mamlambo is associated with deep waters and is believed to inhabit rivers and lakes. His legend has persisted in the oral tradition of Zulu communities, being passed down from generation to generation as an integral part of local culture and beliefs.

Physical and Character Description:

The physical representation of the Mamlambo varies in different accounts, but it is commonly described as a large, snake-like or reptile-like creature with a scaly body and sharp fangs. Its presence is closely linked to water, and it is said that it has the ability to control and manipulate the waters of rivers and lakes. Some legends also attribute to him the ability to change shape.

In terms of character, the Mamlambo is considered a dangerous and fearsome creature. It is associated with misfortune and is believed to cause harm to those who do not respect the waters or invade its territory.

Place of Appearance:

The legends of the Mamlambo come mainly from the Zulu regions in South Africa, where the river and water have significant importance in daily life and cultural beliefs. The Mamlambo is believed to inhabit areas with deep and remote waters.

Main Cultural Aspects:

1. Protector of the Waters: Although the Mamlambo is feared, it is also considered a protector of the waters. Their role includes maintaining balance and harmony in the aquatic world.

2. Rituals and Offerings: In some Zulu communities, rituals and offerings are performed to appease the Mamlambo and seek its favor and protection. These rituals often involve the presentation of gifts in the waters.

Opinions and Theories:

The figure of the Mamlambo is deeply rooted in the beliefs and mythologies of the Zulu communities. Although not considered a tangible physical creature, its presence in oral tradition serves as a reminder of the spiritual connection to nature and the importance of respecting the waters.

From a cultural perspective, the Mamlambo reflects the understanding of duality in nature: a being that can be both protective and dangerous, depending on how it is treated.

5 Curiosities about Mamlambo:

1. Influence on Zulu Culture: The Mamlambo is not only part of Zulu legends, but has also left its mark on the region's contemporary culture, influencing literature, art and music.

2. Association with Misfortune: The presence of the Mamlambo is believed to be linked with misfortune and tragedy, especially if it is provoked or disrespected.

3. Variants in the Story: Different Zulu communities can have variations in the stories of the Mamlambo, which highlights the cultural diversity and adaptation of the legend over time.

4. Connection with Other Mythical Beings: In some narratives, the Mamlambo is associated with other mythical beings from Zulu mythology, expanding the richness of local folklore.

5. Moral Teachings: In addition to their role in explaining natural phenomena, Mamlambo legends often convey moral teachings about respect for nature and the importance of living in harmony with the aquatic environment.

THE LEGEND OF ALUX

The Alux is a mythical creature belonging to Mayan mythology in Mexico and parts of Central America. Described as a small being, similar to an elf or earth spirit, the Alux is considered a supernatural being with the ability to influence people's daily lives. His legend persists in the oral traditions of the Mayan communities, being transmitted as an essential part of the rich regional mythology.

Physical and Character Description:

The physical representation of the Alux may vary in different accounts, but it is commonly described as a small, miniature man-like being with humanoid characteristics. He is often depicted in traditional clothing and attributes that reflect his connection to nature. The Alux has the ability to change size and become invisible, allowing it to move stealthily.

In terms of character, the Alux is known for its duality. Both playful and protective qualities as well as mischief and malice are attributed to him. Some legends consider him a guardian of nature, while others warn of his ability to cause trouble if offended.

Place of Appearance:

The legends of the Alux come mainly from regions where Mayan communities have had a historical presence, such as Mexico and parts of Central America. The Alux is believed to inhabit natural areas, such as forests, jungles and caves.

Main Cultural Aspects:

1. Guardian of Nature: The Alux is considered a guardian of nature, and some Mayan communities perform rituals and offerings to earn its favor and protection.

2. Relationship with the Earth: Alux is believed to have a special connection with the earth and fertility. Its presence is associated with the prosperity of the land and crops.

Opinions and Theories:

From a cultural perspective, the Alux is an essential figure in Mayan mythology and reflects this culture's relationship with nature and the spiritual world. Although it is not considered a physical creature in reality, its influence is palpable in the beliefs and daily practices of some Mayan communities.

5 Curiosities about the Alux:

1. Offerings and Rituals: To gain the favor of the Alux, some Mayan communities perform rituals and offerings, such as leaving small gifts or food in specific places.

2. Protector of Captives: According to some legends, the Alux can be a protector of people who have been kidnapped by evil beings, helping them escape and return to their homes.

3. Regional Names: Although the term "Alux" is commonly used, different regions may have specific local names for this mythical creature.

4. Sacred Constructions: It is believed that the Alux can inhabit sacred constructions, such as pyramids and ancient temples. Their connection to these historical sites adds layers of meaning to their mythology.

5. Taboos and Precautions: There are specific taboos and precautions related to Alux in some Mayan communities. People are warned to avoid certain actions so as not to offend these beings and face negative consequences.

THE LEGEND OF THE ORANG MAWAS:

The Orang Mawas, also known as "Jungle Man", is a mythical creature that is part of the mythology of some communities in Malaysia and Indonesia, especially in the jungle regions of Borneo. Described as a large, hairy hominid, the Orang Mawas has captured the imagination of people in the region and sparked speculation about the possibility of the existence of an unidentified primate.

Physical and Character Description:

The figure of the Orang Mawas is described as a large hominid, similar to a humanoid ape. It is attributed with thick fur that covers its body, and its appearance is often compared to that of an orangutan or gigantopithecus. His height is said to exceed that of average humans.

In terms of character, the legends vary. Some describe the Orang Mawas as a shy and evasive creature that shy away from human presence, while others suggest that it can be aggressive if it feels threatened. It is believed to inhabit the deep, remote jungles of Borneo, adding an air of mystery to its legend.

Place of Appearance:

Stories of the Orang Mawas come primarily from the jungle regions of Borneo, which encompass parts of Malaysia and Indonesia. These creatures are said to inhabit remote and hard-to-access forested areas, contributing to the dearth of tangible evidence.

Main Cultural Aspects:

1. Jungle Creature: The Orang Mawas is considered a jungle creature, adapted to life in dense and isolated jungle habitats.

2. Connection with Local Legends: Some local communities consider the Orang Mawas as part of their local mythologies and include it in their traditional narratives.

Opinions and Theories:

From a scientific point of view, there is no conclusive evidence to support the existence of the Orang Mawas. Although legends persist and some anecdotal accounts have emerged over the years, the lack of solid physical evidence has led many to consider him more of a mythological figure than an actual biological creature.

5 Curiosities about the Orang Mawas:

1. Comparisons with Bigfoot: The figure of the Orang Mawas has been compared to that of Bigfoot in North America due to similarities in the descriptions of large, hairy creatures in both regions.

2. Testimonies and Sightings: Over the years, there have been several testimonies and informal sightings of the Orang Mawas, but none have provided conclusive evidence of its existence.

3. Mystery in the Jungles of Borneo: The jungles of Borneo are known for their biological diversity and challenging terrain, adding an element of mystery to the search for the Orang Mawas.

4. Interest in Cryptozoology: The Orang Mawas has sparked interest in cryptozoology, the study of legendary or unknown animals. However, the lack of evidence has led to scientific skepticism.

5. Impact on Popular Culture: Despite the lack of scientific evidence, the Orang Mawas has left its mark on the popular culture of the region, appearing in stories, books and discussions of local folklore and cryptozoology.

THE LEGEND OF THE HOPKINSVILLE GOBLIN

The Hopkinsville Goblin, also known as the "Kelly-Hopkinsville Incident", is an event that has become part of ufology and popular culture. Occurring in 1955 in Kelly, Kentucky, this incident involved an encounter with supposed extraterrestrial creatures or goblins by a group of people. Although logical explanations have been proposed, the case has persisted as an unsolved mystery.

Physical and Character Description:

According to witness accounts, the creatures described in the Kelly-Hopkinsville incident were small, with large heads, large, luminous eyes, pointed ears, and long arms. They were said to be silver or metallic in color, and moved agilely. Although the description is similar to that of extraterrestrial beings, the interpretation of the creatures varies depending on perspectives.

Regarding their behavior, it was reported that these creatures were prowling around the property where the incident occurred, generating fear and leading witnesses to fire shots to repel them.

Place of Appearance:

The Kelly-Hopkinsville incident took place on a farm near the town of Kelly in the US state of Kentucky. The property belonged to the Sutton family, who reported the encounter with the creatures.

Main Cultural Aspects:

1. Influence on Ufology: The Hopkinsville Goblin case has influenced ufology and has become a reference point for those interested in close encounters of the third kind.

2. Perceptions and Debate: Interpretations of the incident vary. Some see it as an extraterrestrial encounter, while others suggest more earthly explanations, such as the presence of owls.

Opinions and Theories:

The official explanation proposed by some researchers and skeptics suggests that the creatures sighted could have been owls. The fear reaction and nighttime aspect of the incident could have contributed to visual misinterpretations. Others suggest it may have been a social phenomenon, with alcohol consumption and general fear contributing to the creation of the story.

Despite alternative theories, the Hopkinsville Goblin case has maintained its place in popular culture and continues to be the subject of interest and debate.

5 Curiosities about the Hopkinsville Goblin:

1. Intensity of Incident: The encounter at Kelly's farm is reported to have been particularly intense, with witnesses alleging that the creatures were shot several times with no apparent effect.

2. Official Investigation: Although there was no conclusive physical evidence, the case was investigated by police officers and members of the army, who found no obvious explanations.

3. Influence on Popular Culture: The incident has been referenced and reinterpreted in numerous works of fiction, television shows, and films, cementing its place in popular culture.

4. Community Reactions: Following the incident, the local Kelly community experienced an increase in media attention and visits from curious onlookers and paranormal enthusiasts.

5. Connection to Other Sightings: The Hopkinsville Goblin case has occasionally been linked to other close encounters and sightings of similar creatures, creating a larger narrative in ufology.

THE LEGEND OF AHOOL

The Ahool is a mythical creature that is part of Indonesian mythology, specifically on the island of Java. Described as a giant bat, the Ahool has been the subject of local stories and legends that place it in the forests and jungles of the region. Although the creature has been mentioned in several narratives, its existence has not been supported by conclusive evidence.

Physical and Character Description:

The Ahool is described as a large bat, with a wingspan that is believed to exceed three metres. Its appearance includes large eyes and pointed ears, common characteristics in many stories about giant bats. It is said to make a distinctive sound, similar to an "a-hool", which has given it its name.

In terms of behavior, the Ahool is believed to be nocturnal and feeds on small animals in the jungle. Its existence has been the subject of speculation and debate, as there is no solid evidence to support claims of sightings.

Place of Appearance:

The legends of Ahool come mainly from Java, the most populated island in Indonesia. It is said to live in the dense and remote jungles of the region, far from human presence.

Main Cultural Aspects:

1. Nocturnal Creature: The Ahool is considered a nocturnal creature, which adds to its mysterious nature. Stories often link it with darkness and dense jungle.

2. Culturally Relevant: Although the existence of the Ahool is not supported by scientific evidence, the creature has left its mark on legends and local culture, being the subject of discussion and speculation.

Opinions and Theories:

From a scientific perspective, there is no solid evidence to support the existence of the Ahool. Many experts suggest that the stories may be based on misunderstandings of common bat sightings, whose characteristics may be exaggerated in local narratives.

The lack of conclusive physical evidence has led to the Ahool being considered more of a mythological or folkloric figure than an actual biological creature.

5 Curiosities about Ahool:

1. Comparison with Other Cryptids: The Ahool has been compared to other similar cryptids, such as the Kongamato in Africa, which is also described as a giant bat.

2. Appearances in Literature: The figure of Ahool has

appeared in various literary works, both local and international, contributing to its presence in popular culture.

3. Possible Influence on Fantasy Literature: The creature has captured the imagination of writers and creators, serving as inspiration for elements of fantasy and science fiction literature.

4. Richness of Details in the Legends: Although descriptions vary, legends of the Ahool often include specific details about their appearance, behavior and habitat, enriching the folkloric narrative.

5. Continuing Mystery: Despite advances in science and exploration, the Ahool remains an unsolved mystery, maintaining its place in Java's rich tradition of legends and myths.

THE LEGEND OF LOVELAND FROGMAN

The Loveland Frogman is a legendary creature that is part of urban mythology in Loveland, Ohio, USA. Although its existence is not supported by solid evidence, the story of the Loveland Frogman has persisted over the years, generating speculation and debates about the possibility of their presence in the area.

Physical and Character Description:

The Loveland Frogman is described as an amphibian-like creature, with an appearance that combines frog and humanoid characteristics. He is said to have green or grayish skin, bulging eyes, and in some versions of the story, humanoid features such as hands with webbed fingers are attributed to him. The creature is believed to be bipedal and moves similar to a frog or lizard.

In terms of behavior, legends suggest that the Loveland Frogman has been sighted near bodies of water and tends to avoid human presence. Shy and elusive behaviors are attributed to him.

Place of Appearance:

The Loveland Frogman stories come primarily from Loveland, Ohio, a city located along the Little Miami River. Sightings have been reported near water areas and along local roads.

Main Cultural Aspects:

1. Association with Water: The Loveland Frogman is closely associated with bodies of water, which has led to speculation about its possible habitat and amphibian behavior.

2. Night Encounters: Many sightings of the Loveland Frogman have been reported at night, contributing to the mysterious atmosphere of the legend.

Opinions and Theories:

From a scientific perspective, there is no solid evidence to support the existence of the Loveland Frogman. Some suggest that the sightings may be explained by misunderstandings of local animals, such as toads, frogs, or even people in costume. The lack of conclusive physical evidence has led to the creature being considered more of a mythological figure or urban legend than an actual biological entity.

5 Curiosities about the Loveland Frogman:

1. Roadside Encounters: Some accounts of the Loveland Frogman involve encounters on local roads, where the creature is sighted while crossing or resting near the road.

2. Years of Sightings: Reports of sightings of the Loveland Frogman date back to the 1950s and have continued sporadically over the years.

3. Inclusion in Popular Culture: The legend has been incorporated into local popular culture, being the subject of discussions, events and references in the Loveland community.

4. Variants in Description: Over the years, there have been variations in descriptions of the Loveland Frogman, adding an element of ambiguity to the legend.

5. Debate between Believers and Skeptics: The story of the Loveland Frogman has generated debates between those who believe in its existence and those who see it as a folkloric story with no basis in reality.

THE LEGEND OF THE MANTIS MAN

The Mantis Man is a legendary figure who has captured the imagination of those interested in the paranormal and the unexplainable. Described as a humanoid creature with features similar to those of a praying mantis, the Mantis Man has been the subject of reports and accounts suggesting close encounters and sightings. Although the veracity of these stories is questionable, the legend of the Mantis Man persists as an enigma in paranormal culture.

Physical and Character Description:

The Mantis Man is commonly described as a humanoid creature with distinctive features of a praying mantis, an insect known for its elongated front legs and leaf-like resemblance. It is said to have a bipedal stance and compound eyes similar to those of a mantis. Its appearance is often associated with a mix between insect and human.

In terms of behavior, accounts vary. Some stories suggest that the Mantis Man is a peaceful and observant figure, while others describe him as more intrusive and unnerving. Encounters with the Mantis Man have been reported in different contexts, from rural to urban areas.

Place of Appearance:

Sightings and encounters with the Mantis Man have been reported in various locations, although there is no specific location associated with the creature. The stories have emerged in different regions of the world, adding a global dimension to the legend.

Main Cultural Aspects:

1. Association with the Paranormal: The Mantis Man is commonly associated with the paranormal realm and close encounters with beings of unknown origin.

2. Similarities with Other Creatures: The figure of the Mantis Man shares similarities with other legends of insectoid humanoids present in various cultures, reflecting recurring patterns in global folklore.

Opinions and Theories:

The legend of the Mantis Man is widely considered to be part of urban mythology and stories of close encounters with extraterrestrial or interdimensional beings. The lack of conclusive physical evidence has led many to view it as an expression of human creativity, influenced by cultural phenomena and interest in the paranormal.

Theories regarding encounters with the Mantis Man are often intertwined with ufology and belief in the presence of beings from other worlds or dimensions that interact with humanity.

5 Curiosities about the Mantis Man:

1. Variety in Descriptions: Although the main figure is that of a humanoid praying mantis, there are variations in the descriptions of the Mantis Man according to reports and testimonies.

2. Encounters in Different Contexts: Encounters with the Mantis Man have been reported in various situations, from rural areas and forests to urban areas, adding an additional layer of mystery to the legend.

3. Relationship to Extraterrestrial Abduction: In some accounts, the Mantis Man is associated with extraterrestrial abduction experiences, suggesting a connection between the figure and the ufological narrative.

4. Influence on Popular Culture: Although the legend is not as well known as some other figures in folklore, the Mantis Man has influenced popular culture and has appeared in discussions about the paranormal.

5. Interest in the Paranormal: Encounters with the Mantis Man are often linked to communities interested in the paranormal, ufology and unexplained mysteries, generating debate and speculation in these circles.

THE LEGEND OF THE FLATWOODS MONSTER

The Flatwoods Monster, also known as the "Green Stalker" or "Flatwoods Monster", is a legendary creature that has left its mark on the urban mythology of West Virginia, United States. The incident involving him took place in 1952, generating reports of sightings and becoming part of popular culture. Although various explanations have been proposed, the legend of the Flatwoods Monster persists as an unsolved mystery.

Physical and Character Description:

The Flatwoods Monster is described as a tall creature, with a humanoid appearance and a heart-shaped or heart-shaped head. It is said to have luminous eyes and a body wrapped in a kind of flowing robe or garment, which is often described as green. Its appearance is described as alien or extraterrestrial, and its presence has been associated with UFO sightings.

In terms of behavior, initial reports describe the Flatwoods Monster as an entity that appeared suddenly and then retreated without directly interacting with witnesses. Sightings are commonly associated with ufological phenomena and close encounters.

Place of Appearance:

The Flatwoods Monster incident took place in Flatwoods, West Virginia, specifically in the hills of Braxton County. The creature was sighted after several witnesses reported a shiny object falling in the area.

Main Cultural Aspects:

1. Link to UFO Phenomena: The Flatwoods Monster has been associated with UFO sightings and extraterrestrial phenomena, contributing to its place in UFO culture.

2. Impact on Local Culture: The incident has left a lasting mark on the local culture of Flatwoods, which has adopted the figure of the Flatwoods Monster as part of its identity.

Opinions and Theories:

Explanations for the Flatwoods Monster incident vary. Some suggest it could have been a case of a large owl sighting, while others link it to unusual atmospheric phenomena or even secret military experiments. The lack of conclusive physical evidence has led to the case being the subject of debate and speculation.

From the skeptical point of view, it has been noted that the incident occurred during a time when UFO reports were on the rise, which could have influenced the witnesses' perception and interpretation of the event.

5 Curiosities about the Flatwoods Monster:

1. Monument in Flatwoods: In honor of the Flatwoods Monster, a monument was erected in Flatwoods, West Virginia, which has become an attraction for those interested in the paranormal.

2. Influence on Popular Culture: The Flatwoods Monster incident has been referenced in television shows, documentaries and films related to the paranormal and UFOs.

3. Variations in Description: Over the years, there have been variations in descriptions of the Flatwoods Monster, which has contributed to the ambiguity and controversy surrounding the incident.

4. Connection to Other Sightings: The Flatwoods incident has occasionally been linked to other sightings of UFOs and similar creatures in the region, creating a broader narrative in ufology.

5. Continuing Mystery: Despite the research and proposed theories, the Flatwoods Monster incident remains an unsolved mystery and a source of fascination for those interested in the paranormal and close encounters.

THE LEGEND OF NINGEN

The Ningen is a mythical creature that is part of Japanese mythology and urban legends that circulate around the oceans of the southern hemisphere, especially in Antarctica. Described as a humanoid marine being of gigantic proportions and anthropomorphic appearance, the Ningen has generated speculation and debate around its existence. Although the lack of solid evidence questions its reality, the legend persists as part of modern culture and the fascination with the unknown.

Physical and Character Description:

The Ningen is described as a marine creature of colossal proportions, with an appearance that combines human and marine mammal characteristics. Its skin resembles that of a whale or dolphin, and is said to lack fins and scales, having a smooth surface similar to human skin. The creature has humanoid limbs and, in some accounts, facial details such as eyes and mouth are mentioned.

In terms of behavior, the Ningen legends do not provide specific details, as much of the narrative focuses on visual sightings and surprise at the appearance of such a large creature in the ocean.

Place of Appearance:

Reports and legends about the Ningen have arisen mainly in the Antarctic region, where these giant creatures are said to emerge in remote, cold waters. Stories have also circulated in other areas of the southern hemisphere, especially in deep and little-explored waters.

Main Cultural Aspects:

1. Modern Phenomenon: Unlike many mythical creatures with historical roots, the Ningen is a more modern phenomenon, associated with the era of polar exploration and improved information technology.

2. Connection with the Unknown: The legend of the Ningen reflects the human fascination with the unknown in the oceans and the possibility that giant and mysterious creatures inhabit the deep sea.

Opinions and Theories:

The lack of solid physical evidence and the nature of the reports, often based on visual encounters and anecdotal testimony, have led to the Ningen being considered more of a cultural phenomenon and urban legend than an actual biological creature.

Explanations for the Ningen sightings vary, from the possibility of misinterpretations of icebergs or conventional marine animals to the idea that the creature could have paranormal or extraterrestrial origins.

5 Curiosities about Ningen:

1. Visual Sightings: Reports on the Ningen are often based on visual sightings from ships or aircraft, which adds an element of mystery to the narrative.

2. Variety in Descriptions: Different reports offer variations in the description of the Ningen, which contributes to the lack of clarity about its exact appearance.

3. Cultural Phenomenon: Despite the lack of conclusive evidence, the Ningen legend has influenced popular culture and has become a topic of discussion in communities interested in the paranormal and the marine.

4. Influence on Art: The figure of Ningen has inspired works of art, illustrations and visual representations in contemporary culture, highlighting its impact on human creativity.

5. Scientific Exploration: Although the existence of the Ningen is widely questioned, the legend has sparked interest in scientific exploration of the deep sea and the search for undiscovered life forms in the oceans.

THE LEGEND OF
THE KRAKEN

The Kraken is a legendary creature that has been part of Norse and Scandinavian mythologies, known for being a sea monster of giant proportions and ferocious tentacles. Throughout the centuries, the legend of the Kraken has endured, inspiring fear and curiosity in the minds of sailors and lovers of the supernatural. Although descriptions vary, the image of the Kraken has left an indelible mark on popular culture and marine narratives.

Physical and Character Description:

The Kraken is commonly described as a sea monster of enormous proportions, with massive tentacles that can reach impressive lengths. It is said to live in the depths of the ocean and emerge to catch prey, especially unsuspecting boats and sailors. The Kraken's specific appearance has varied over time, but in general, it is depicted as a terrifying creature with an imposing presence.

In terms of behavior, the Kraken is feared for its ability to sink entire ships with its tentacles and its insatiable voracity. Some legends also suggest that it is capable of creating whirlpools and tidal waves with its movements in the water.

Place of Appearance:

Legends of the Kraken have arisen in Norse and Scandinavian mythologies, with mention of this creature in ancient texts such as Icelandic sagas and medieval maps. Although the stories originated in northern Europe, narratives about similar sea monsters are found in various cultures around the world.

Main Cultural Aspects:

1. Symbol of Marine Mystery: The Kraken has become a symbol of the mystery and danger of the deep sea, fueling the human imagination about the unknown in the oceans.

2. Influence on Literature and Art: The legend of the Kraken has inspired classic literary works such as Alfred Tennyson's "The Legend of the Kraken" and has appeared in numerous artistic representations throughout history.

Opinions and Theories:

Although the legend of the Kraken has been an integral part of Norse mythology, modern science does not support the existence of a sea monster such as that described in ancient narratives. Various theories have been proposed to explain the Kraken's stories, ranging from misunderstandings of observations of real animals to unusual natural phenomena.

Some scientists suggest that historical sightings of

"krakens" could have been inspired by encounters with giant squid, which are real animals but rarely seen in their natural habitat.

5 Curiosities about the Kraken:

1. Giant Squid: It is believed that the Kraken sightings could have been influenced by encounters with giant squid, which can reach considerable sizes in real life.

2. Presence in Popular Culture: The Kraken has left its mark on popular culture, appearing in films, books, video games and other entertainment media.

3. Literary Inspiration: The figure of the Kraken has been a source of literary inspiration, standing out in works such as "20,000 Leagues Under the Sea" by Jules Verne and "Pirates of the Caribbean" by Disney.

4. Possible Influence on the Evolution of Marine Legends: The legend of the Kraken has influenced other narratives of sea monsters in various cultures, contributing to the development of myths and legends related to the unknown in the oceans.

5. Myths and Reality: Although the Kraken is largely considered a myth, science has revealed the existence of surprising sea creatures, adding a touch of reality to ancient legends of monsters in the ocean.

www.ingramcontent.com/pod-product-compliance
Lightning Source LLC
Chambersburg PA
CBHW050831260726

48660CB00006B/2186